# MADE IN GOD'S IMAGE 31-DAY DEVOTIONAL
## VOLUME 1

Cultivating a Divine Perception

C. ORVILLE MCLEISH

**Made in God's Image Devotional | Volume 1.**
Copyright © 2018. C. Orville McLeish

All rights reserved. No portion of this book may be reproduced, stored in a retrieval system, or transmitted in any form or by any means – electronic, mechanical, photocopy, recording, scanning, or other – except for a brief quotation in critical reviews or articles, without the prior written permission of the publisher or author.

Published by:

ISBN: 978-1-949343-20-5 (paperback)

ISBN: 978-1-949343-21-2 (ebook)

Scripture taken from the New King James Version®. Copyright © 1982 by Thomas Nelson. Used by permission. All rights reserved.

Scriptures taken from the Holy Bible, New International Version®, NIV®. Copyright © 1973, 1978, 1984, 2011 by Biblica, Inc.™ Used by permission of Zondervan. All rights reserved worldwide. www.zondervan.com. The "NIV" and "New International Version" are trademarks registered in the United States Patent and Trademark Office by Biblica, Inc.™

Unless otherwise indicated, all scripture quotations are from The Holy Bible, English Standard Version (ESV). Copyright 2001 by Crossway Bibles, a division of Good News Publishers. Used by permission. All rights reserved.

Scripture quotations marked NLT are taken from the Holy Bible, New Living Translation, copyright 1996, 2004, 2007. Used by permission of Tyndale House Publishers, Inc. Carol Stream, Illinois 60188. All rights reserved.

Scripture quotations marked KJV are from the Holy Bible, King James Version (Authorized Version). First published in 1611. Quoted from the KJV Classic Reference Bible, Copyright 1983, by The Zondervan Corporation.

Scripture quotations marked NASB are taken from the New American Standard Bible, Copyright 1960, 1962, 1963, 1968, 1971, 1972, 1973, 1975, 1977, 1995 by The Lockman Foundation. Used by permission.

Scripture taken from the Holy Bible: International Standard Version®. Copyright © 1996-forever by The ISV Foundation. ALL RIGHTS RESERVED INTERNATIONALLY. Used by permission.

# Table of Contents

Introduction ..................................................... 1

DAY 1: Made in God's Image ................... 3

DAY 2: We Are Partakers of God's Divine Nature ..................... 6

DAY 4: As He (Jesus) Is, So Are We (Part 1) ......................................... 10

DAY 5: Made in God's Likeness ............. 12

DAY 6: Awakening God-Consciousness (Part I) ............................................ 14

DAY 7: Our Words Create Our World . 18

DAY 8: The Secret Place (Part I) ............ 21

DAY 9: Operating in Rest ....................... 24

DAY 10: Taking Your Seat of Rest ........... 27

DAY 11: The Secret Place (Part II) ........... 30

DAY 12: As He (Jesus) Is, So Are We (Part 2) ......................................... 33

DAY 13: Becoming Love ........................... 35

DAY 14: Awakening God-Consciousness (Part 2) ......................................... 37

DAY 15: The Kingdom Of God Is Within (Part 1) ....................... 41

| DAY 16: | Creating Balance in the World ... 44 |
| --- | --- |
| DAY 17: | The Power of Silence ................... 48 |
| DAY 18: | Eyes to See ..................................... 51 |
| DAY 19: | The Currency of a Supernatural Life ........................ 54 |
| DAY 20: | When Our Faith Doesn't Work ... 57 |
| DAY 21: | The Kingdom of God Is Within (Part 2) ............................ 60 |
| DAY 22: | Expectation Versus Faith .......... 63 |
| DAY 23: | Overcoming the Enemy (Self) .... 67 |
| DAY 24: | Union With God ......................... 70 |
| DAY 25: | Shifting Perspective – Renewing the Mind .................... 74 |
| DAY 26: | Untethering From the Church System ............................ 77 |
| DAY 27: | Untethering From the World System .............................. 81 |
| DAY 28: | Walking in the Spirit ................. 85 |
| DAY 29: | Taking Your Seat With Christ .... 88 |
| DAY 30: | Immortality Now ........................ 91 |
| DAY 31: | To Him Who Overcomes ........... 95 |
| About The Author .......................................... 99 | |

# Introduction

I have a great mentor, and I have sat under hours of his teachings on Kingdom Mysteries/Christian Spirituality and still feel like I haven't begun to scratch the surface. Of course, the freedom to share everything I learn is not there because I have yet to live out much of the knowledge I have acquired through study, listening to hours of teaching, and reading dozens of books, plus my own intuition and secret conversations with God at different intervals of my life. I don't have all the answers, nor do I pretend to know a lot.

By the time I finished writing this devotional, I had a barrage of new questions and no answers. As I learn and grow, I invite you to join me on this journey. It is indeed an interesting one, and for every question answered, a dozen unanswered questions will take its place. It is just the nature of the journey, so enjoy the ride. The priority is not to answer your questions, but to expand your mind so more of God can seep in – expanding your capacity to become a life-giving principle and an agent of change and spiritual transformation in the world you live in today.

Most Christians today want to escape the world, but God is looking for a few brave men and women who will choose to stick around and partner with Him in the transfiguration of fallen creation.

# DAY 1:

# MADE IN GOD'S IMAGE

Scripture:

> *"Let us make man in Our image, after Our likeness..."* (Genesis 1:26 – KJV)

What does it mean to be made in the image of God? To answer this question, I found a fascinating article on the Focus on the Family website. I found the exposition so profound that I would prefer to quote it than paraphrase it:

> "...the Image of God is not so much something that man *bears* as something that man *is*. Biblical scholar D. J. A. Clines, in his groundbreaking article "The Image of God in Man" (*Tyndale Bulletin* 19, 1968, 53-103) argues that the Hebrew preposition *be* ("in") in the phrases *betsalmenu*, "in our image," and *betsalmo*, "in his image" (Genesis 1:27), should be taken as an instance of "*beth* essentiae" or "*beth* of the essence." We realize that this may be difficult to grasp if you don't

know any Hebrew, but the point is that the grammar favors the translation "God created man *as* His image" over "God created man *in* His image." As Cline puts it in his concluding remarks: "Thus we may say that according to Genesis 1, man does not *have* the image of God, nor is he made *in* the image of God, but *is himself* the image of God." Humankind, then, was created to *be* a "copy" or a "graphic image" of the Creator – a *formal, visible, and understandable representation* of who God is and what He is really like."[1]

What I like about this author's conclusion is that it now makes sense why God would be so vested in mankind. If we are His expressed image, then it would make sense that if we fell from grace, He would do everything possible to redeem us. This shows just how valuable you are to God.

---

1 https://www.focusonthefamily.com/family-q-and-a/faith/what-it-means-to-be-made-in-the-image-of-god

**Prayer:**

Father, forgive me for thinking I was worthless and had no value. I now see why You would be so mindful of us, why You would even consider us, because You truly value our existence. May You open my eyes to recognize the truth about who You are and who I am in You, in Jesus' Name. Amen.

# DAY 2:

# WE ARE PARTAKERS OF GOD'S DIVINE NATURE

It was Peter who said,

> And because of his glory and excellence, he has given us great and precious promises. These are the promises that enable you to share his divine nature and escape the world's corruption caused by human desires. (2 Peter 1:4 – NLT)

Now, I need you to consider the word, 'share.' *Share* in this version replaces 'partake' in the King James Version. The original word is *'koinonos,'* which means *'companion, fellowship, partaker, partner.'* I think many Christians have spent so much time arguing how 'not like' God we are that we miss the invitation that has been extended to us. We can creep into God and live our lives from that place, participating in the very fabric of His being. This is how miracles, signs, and wonders break out around us, for such things flow from the nature of who God is. Those who are in God, by virtue of a new birth, participate in His nature.

God is not like us, but we were made like Him, initially. The invitation is for us to share the very essence of what makes Him God. If we accept, we can participate in a reality that is not confined to matter, space, or time. In Christ, we can live out of the future, as David did, for he partook of the Holy Spirit before the Holy Spirit was given. It is an invitation, not an automatic reality, which means we need to grow into it by our own choice and will.

**Prayer:**

Father, thank You for what You have made available to us, through Jesus Christ. I admit that such an invitation to participate in Your nature is a bit overwhelming and surreal, but I accept that it was Your intention from the beginning when You created man from the dust. So, Lord, my answer to Your invitation is a resounding, YES!

# DAY 3:

# GOD'S ORIGINAL INTENT

Scripture:

> In the beginning, God said, *"Let us make man in our image, after our likeness... So God created man in His own image, in the image of God created He him; male and female created He them."* (Genesis 1:26-27 – KJV)

Man fell from his original state, which had an adverse cosmic effect on all creation. The word *'fell'* suggests a descent from our original form, function, structure, and faculty. We could no longer be identified in our original form. The process of faith in Yeshua (Jesus) is to take us back to where we fell from; it's a transmutative, transfigurative process that seeks to complete the full restoration of our bodies back to its divine essence, allowing it to do all that it was made to do.

The reality is, we were made (body, soul, and spirit) 'LIKE GOD.' In other words, our fallen body is not what it is supposed to be, yet. Our spirit and soul are renewed because, in Christ, we have been made into a new creation (2 Corinthians 5:17). It is only our body that is left to come into the fullness of who we were created to be. That is why our doctrine is all about the resurrection and renewal of the body. What we may not realize, or are reluctant to accept, is that the spiritual transformation of the body can take place without us physically dying. It's called 'Transfiguration.'

**Prayer:**

Father, as Jesus Christ, Your Son, was transfigured on the Mount before the eyes of three of His Disciples, I recognize that it is recorded to reveal the future transformation of believers. Paul says we will not all die, but we will all be changed (1 Corinthians 15:51). I break the covenant and agreement that I have made with death, and I yoke myself to Your original intent for my life and body, in the Name of Jesus.

## DAY 4:

# AS HE (JESUS) IS, SO ARE WE (PART 1)

Scripture:

> *By this, love is perfected with us, so that we may have confidence in the day of judgment; because as He is, so also are we in this world. (1 John 4:17 – NASB)*

There is so much to say on this topic that I decided to break this devotional into several parts. I pray that by reading this, your perception of YOU and GOD will change. Every believer needs to grow into the fullness of Christ until we are fully conformed to His image. We were always meant to become like Jesus and function in the same capacity. We miss the fact that the journey of faith is supposed to take us from where we are to where we need to be.

In talking to a friend, I realized that the church culture, structure, and demands have caused many believers to get stuck. Our issues become something we sweep under the carpet in order to perform the duties that rest on our shoulders. In doing this, our efforts become performance-based and we seek accolades and affirmations from men. In reality, we end up hiding our hearts from God. He never gets access to what truly matters; therefore, we don't experience His transforming power. All the issues we face today are a matter of the condition of the human heart. We are already like Jesus in potential, but we now need to endure the process of realizing who we are in knowledge, understanding, and experience.

**Prayer:**

Father, as I begin this journey to understanding who I am in You, I pray that I will have the wisdom and the courage to truly open my heart to You. I realize that the thoughts of my heart are not entirely pure – that I struggle to love and tolerate people, and understand Your love for me and for humanity. In essence, Father, I just don't get it. May my journey to You, to fellowship and experience in Your manifested presence, begin now, in Jesus' Name.

# DAY 5:

# MADE IN GOD'S LIKENESS

Scripture:

> "Let us make man in Our image, after Our likeness..." (Genesis 1:26 – KJV)

What does it mean to be made in the likeness of God? It can be scary to think that humanity was initially created to look and function like God. But we must realize that it was God's intention, not ours. We are prone to view life and reality from a fallen perspective, which usually strips something of its real value and nature.

Recently, I had an encounter that taught me a very valuable lesson. I realize that there are different versions of ourselves that we can pursue. There is the lower, fallen aspect, where we can live out every day of our lives just to eat, sleep, and have sex. For others, it is eat, work, sleep, and have sex. But there are higher forms of self that can be pursued, for example, our likeness to God, which is embedded in our DNA, but must be activated, cultured, practiced, and matured. It takes time to do this and requires a conscious effort on our part.

Each of us must decide which aspect of our self we want to cultivate and build up. Will we focus on our animalistic nature (by virtue of the fall) or our divine nature, which Jesus came in the flesh to restore?

**Prayer:**

Father, life is filled with choices, and I am in desperate need of help to keep making the right decision. I don't want to pursue what was never Your intention for me to pursue. I want to become like You again in form and function. I want to know what it looks like and feels like to be like You again. I feel far from the mark and recognize that it will be a journey to get there, most times even swimming against the tide, but with Your help, I know I can do it, in Jesus' Name.

# DAY 6:

# AWAKENING GOD-CONSCIOUSNESS (PART I)

Scripture:

> Wherefore he saith, awake thou that sleepest, and arise from the dead, and Christ shall give thee light. See then that ye walk circumspectly, not as fools, but as wise. (Ephesians 5:14-15 – KJV)

The church is sleeping. We sing, *"Awake, Zion, Awake,"* yet there is not much awareness of the presence of God in our daily lives. Our every prayer is a war against demons, witches, warlocks, and all kinds of evil entities. If our worship is genuinely about getting into the presence of God, I don't see how we can do that and then turn around and start talking to demons.

Consider Joseph. What made him choose to run from a beautiful woman who desired him? Not many men run these days, and if we are honest with ourselves, within us lies the possibility of both good and evil, existing simultaneously at all times. It is inherent that when we think of doing good, we find the presence of evil as well. What has defeated us over the years is our denial of it. We think if we say it is not so, then, magically, it will not be true. Which one of us grown men have not found ourselves looking at a woman with inappropriate thoughts? Who has not contemplated the worst possible scenario when we are offended by someone or when a bad driver crosses us on the road? We have entertained bad thoughts for someone we don't like. We wish they would trip and fall in full view of a crowd of people or that some calamity would befall them as a payback for something cruel they said or did. Thus is the nature of man, more specifically, a sleeping believer.

There is a reason Jesus told His disciples, *"Watch and pray that you don't fall into temptation. The spirit is willing; the flesh is weak"* (Matthew 26:41). The spirit is righteous; the flesh pulls us toward unrighteousness. We are both, at the same time. Joseph had a God-consciousness, which enables one to see God above the very things we are tempted with. It is a difficult scenario, and one that many men and women have failed, even among the clergy. We know the stories.

There is a call for the church to awake. I have observed how focused we are on the demonic; we study the devil, talk about him, curse him, rebuke him, and bind him – and yet our lives do not improve. It just gets worst. We have become experts on the devil but lack the transformational knowledge of God that we so desperately need in this time. How much would our lives change if we stop focusing so much on demons and begin to engage with deep fervor and intention the presence and heart of God?

**Prayer:**

Father, help me to shift my focus to what is pure, lovely, right, virtuous, of a good report, and worthy of praise. Teach me to engage Your presence more than I engage the kingdom of darkness. I want to turn my focus to You, Lord, to engage Your presence more; to understand the angels who encamp around me more; to learn how to worship You in Spirit and in Truth, in Jesus' Name. Amen.

# DAY 7:

# OUR WORDS CREATE OUR WORLD

Scripture:

> Death and life *are* in the power of the tongue, and those who love it will eat its fruit. (Proverbs 18:21 – NKJV)

I see it every day as I observe the world and the people around me. We speak freely, creating the very reality we eventually experience, and yet, there is a failure to connect our experiences to what we uttered with our very powerful tongue. King Solomon was not kidding when he said we possess the power of life and death in our tongue. We have been speaking the reality of our experiences since we learned to speak consciously. The suggestion here is that our experiences – and by extension, the world – cannot change unless we train ourselves to speak a different language or stop speaking.

Every recorded miracle in the Bible has speech attached to it. Even more remarkable was King David's affinity to speak life over himself. He believed in 'self-talk,' so we often read a Psalm that begins with a tone of gloom and despair, but somewhere in the middle, we see David speaking to his soul or the circumstance, and the last verses of that Psalm often ends with praise and thanksgiving, and a total shift in David's perception of the situation he was facing at the time. I believe that is a perfect example for us to follow.

We look at the world, see and hear the news, and daily our hearts sink from some tragic news from somewhere around the world. We don't like the world, and we want to escape it, but not by death. Every generation looks with eager anticipation for Jesus to return and fix everything, but what if the onus is on us to change our world, to fix what is broken, by first changing our speech?

**Prayer:**

Father, thank You that You made us to be just like You. As You spoke the world into existence by the breath of Your words, may You help me also to speak life with every breath, speak life with every word, speak life with every syllable I utter from my lips so the world can begin to be transformed by virtue of what I choose to consciously speak over it, in Jesus' Name. Amen.

# DAY 8:

# THE SECRET PLACE (PART I)

Scripture:

> He that dwelleth in the secret place of the most High shall abide under the shadow of the Almighty. (Psalm 91:1 – KJV)

There is such a placed called the "Secret Place" that I think we overlook. In our present culture, bombarded with distractions, the secret place has been ignored or simply neglected. Yet we somehow still feel qualified, especially as leaders, to stand before people and give them 'God.' What you are actually giving them is you.

God values His secret time with you more than He values your public display and articulation of *(what you believe you know about)* Him. We have missed this in churches, and I believe we often waste our time when we gather, because we really have nothing to give each other. The Bible does say we should not forsake the assembling of ourselves together; it also says where two or three are gathered, Jesus is in the midst. In a family home of two or more, when you gather, that qualifies as the assembling of yourself, which means, we are very guilty of the rest of that verse that says, *"not neglecting to gather together, <u>as some are in the habit of doing</u>, but encouraging each other, and all the more as you see the day approaching"* (Hebrews 10:25 – CSB).

We need to repair our family altars and get back into the habit of assembling to bring encouragement, not gossip, backbiting, spreading rumors, and all that foolishness we frequently do whenever and wherever two or three are gathered. We need to get back to that secret place with God where we walk and talk with Him – heart to heart, soul to soul, and face to face. The truth is – and it will help you to get this – your entire life, ministry, and relationships should flow from the secret place.

Prayer:

Father, forgive me for neglecting what is truly important to You. I get so caught up in the distractions of life and the demands of work and school that I barely find time for our secret and precious time together. When I do, sometimes my mind is so bombarded with all the things I need and want to do that I am agitated, anxious, and can't still my mind enough to hear You. I repent and acknowledge that You are drawing me back to that secret place with You, and instead of resisting, I surrender. Help me find at least one hour out of each day to just be with You, in Jesus' Name. Amen.

# DAY 9:

# OPERATING IN REST

Scripture:

> Be anxious for nothing, but in everything by prayer and supplication, with thanksgiving, let your requests be made known to God; and the peace of God, which surpasses all understanding, will guard your hearts and minds through Christ Jesus. (Philippians 4:6-7 – NKJV)

We can sometimes fill our lives with anxiety, stress, and worry when we face our different circumstances and tests, but God commands a different response. He says, "Don't be anxious" and tells us what to do instead. The result is 'peace.' The original word used for 'peace' is *'eirene,'* which also translates as 'prosperity, quietness, rest.'

The analogy I received by the Spirit is the sun. It is set on a course that it never deviates from and moves in obedience. If you have read *The Book of Enoch*, you will realize that each day, the sun comes through one of six portals in the east and goes through one of six in the west. It follows its path in obedience and never goes off track. What is even more amazing is that if you keep staring at the sun, it doesn't seem to move. Yet, when you look away and look back, it is never in the same position you saw it in previously because there is always movement, but it is movement from a place of rest, which is why science says the sun doesn't move.

Whatever circumstance we face today, we can go through it from the perspective of rest and not agitation. The reality is, agitation and worry produce little to nothing, which is why we sometimes do not learn from those things that are allowed in our life to teach us. There is a reason God says "Don't worry." Worry actually blocks the transformation process of our experiences, and that's not something we want to do because all things work together for good to them that love the Lord.

**Prayer:**

Father, forgive me for responding to my circumstances with agitation, anxiety, and worry. I know this is not what You desire of me. Help me find that place of rest in any storm that I face, so that, like the sun, I can move obediently through my day, through any weather, through any circumstance, and remain unmovable, unshakable, and undeterred in my relentless pursuit to live a life of obedience to Your Word, in Jesus' Name. Amen.

# DAY 10:

# TAKING YOUR SEAT OF REST

Scripture:

> Let us labour therefore to enter into that rest, lest any man fall after the same example of unbelief. (Hebrews 4:11 - KJV)

I sat in my prayer chair, and I was immediately in the Spirit. I saw Jesus, and He gestured toward a chair. I knew He was saying the chair belonged to me, and I should sit, so I sat down in the chair. He came and sat in a similar chair next to mine. I understood what it meant to be seated with Christ, but even more so, I knew I was sitting in my seat of rest. It is from that position we are called to rule and take dominion on the earth.

Someone once came to Jesus, saying they wanted to also do the work of the Father as He was doing. Jesus said, *"This is the only work God wants from you: Believe in the one he has sent"* (John 6:29). So, our labor is one of faith. Hebrews 4 alludes to the alternative to this 'work' being from a place of unbelief. This suggests that our 'church labor' that often leads to stress, many gray hairs, and burnout is because of our unbelief. We still believe we can work our way into heaven, and it is our manual labor that will be rewarded. But we have already been positioned in heaven by the accomplished work on the cross. Jesus has redeemed the sweat of our brows and made our work an exercise of faith.

The Bible says we are "seated with Christ in heavenly places" (Ephesians 2:6), but most of those seats are presently empty because many believers have not yet occupied what rightfully belongs to them.

Prayer:

Father, thank You for providing a seat of rest for me. Thank You that I can be seated with Christ in heavenly places, having access to His mind, His thoughts, and His ways, and I can function on the earth from that place. I ask that You help me to identify my seat, and to occupy it, so my perspective of life can begin to change and I will see life through Your eyes, and react accordingly, in Jesus' Name.

# DAY 11:

# THE SECRET PLACE (PART II)

Scripture:

> He that dwelleth in the secret place of the most High shall abide under the shadow of the Almighty. (Psalm 91:1 – KJV)

There is a secret place that cannot be found outside of ourselves, and it is also the place where God is enthroned, and that is within the believer. We are the temple of the living God, and it is in that temple that we meet with God and communicate effectively.

When Jesus was teaching on praying to the Father effectively, He said this:

> And when you pray, do not be like the hypocrites, for they love to pray standing in the synagogues and on the street corners to be seen by others. Truly I tell you, they have received their reward in full. But when you pray, go into your room, close the door and pray

to your Father, who is unseen. Then your Father, who sees what is done in secret, will reward you. (Matthew 6:5-6 – NIV)

The King James Version uses the word 'closet' instead of 'room.' The original word is *'tam-i'-on,'* which can also be interpreted as 'secret chamber.' God waits for us in this place. He is always present, always eager for us to enter and communicate with Him. This is the place we should operate from as children of God. This is where His voice is heard, known, and obeyed. This is the chamber in which God shares His secrets, and most of the conversations we have with God in this place is not spoken outside the secret place. We are not permitted to share everything God tells us with the world.

If you want to experience personal, spiritual transformation in your life, then you need to shift your focus from a public display of eloquent speech and verbal articulation, for at that place, words are usually chosen and spoken from the perspective of the people who are listening. But in the secret place with

God, we are permitted to speak from our hearts, with our sole focus being on Him, on hearing Him – for only in that place can a true heart-to-heart conversation be had with God.

> Prayer:
>
> Father, forgive me for praying wrongly, when it is clear in Scripture how we ought to pray. There is no greater joy than to hear Your voice and no grander privilege than the opportunity to obey You, so I ask that You will help me to locate this secret chamber that You have established within my being so I can meet You there daily, that when I step out into the world, our secret communication can result in my presence touching lives in the world, for Your glory Lord, in Jesus' Name. Amen.

# DAY 12:

# AS HE (JESUS) IS, SO ARE WE (PART 2)

Scripture:

> By this, love is perfected with us, so that we may have confidence in the day of judgment; because as He is, so also are we in this world. (1 John 4:17 – NASB)

The power of the statement "As Jesus is, so are we" is beyond articulation. We were brought up under the false assumption that while we were made in God's image, by virtue of the fall, we lost our capacity to ever be like God again. This is faulty thinking and a heretic misunderstanding of the purpose of Christ as God being made flesh.

If it is true that Jesus came to restore all things, then what is *'all things'* being restored to? Surely the answer lies prior to the fall that introduced sin into the context of humanity. If all we know then is the result of the fall, and the faulty thinking that accompanies that reality, then truly eye hath not seen, ears have not heard, nor has it entered into the heart of man what God has prepared for those who love Him.

The good news is, if we want to know who we are, then we have to gaze at Christ because He is the prototype of who we were before the fall and who we, believers, are destined to become again. The reality of our true identity then lies both in the past and in the future and is accessible now by the blood of Jesus Christ, which was shed to give us access to what was denied us by the fall.

> **Prayer:**
>
> Father, open my eyes to see Your Truth. Let me not be blinded by faulty thinking and doctrines of men but develop a heart that will seek to know you experientially and from a spiritual perspective. I see now that a greater understanding of who You are will result in a greater understanding of who I am in You, so help me to gaze at Your perfection until my imperfection disappears, in Jesus' Name.

# DAY 13:

# BECOMING LOVE

Scripture:

> Beloved, let us love one another, for love is from God, and whoever loves has been born of God and knows God. Anyone who does not love does not know God, because God is love. (1 John 4:7-8 – ESV)

I had a dream. I was approached by a young lady from my church to pray for her because she was having pain below her breast. For some reason, it shifted from commanding her to be healed to holding her baby in my arms. The baby was in need of prayer too and crying for his mother. I began to sing and the baby quieted down, and then I prayed for the baby to be healed. What was remarkable is that the power I felt leaving my body and entering into the child was 'Love.'

In my studies, I came across this phrase quite often, "Love is more powerful than death." Many say love cannot be defined, and they are right. It is a force that transcends definition because it cannot be contained within human language. If we should consider Scripture, we will come to the conclusion that God is love, and to give love, is to give God. We cannot bring healing to someone we don't love, because Love is what heals. Quite often in Scripture, we see Jesus moved with compassion just prior to performing a miracle.

Today, find someone to love. Look within yourself and identify the areas of compassion you may be feeling for those who are suffering in the world. Do you have a burden for the lost? Do you have a burden for the elderly? Do you have a burden for the terminally ill? Become love in prayer and deed to someone today.

Prayer:

Father, thank You that I do not have to define love, because You are love. In loving others, I open up the reality of heaven to them by showing them Your heart. You first loved us, even when we were sinners. It is Your love, through us, that will heal the world, and I thank You that I am a worthy vessel honored to embody true Love, in Jesus' Name.

# DAY 14:

# AWAKENING GOD-CONSCIOUSNESS (PART 2)

Scripture:

> Wherefore he saith, awake thou that sleepest, and arise from the dead, and Christ shall give thee light. See then that ye walk circumspectly, not as fools, but as wise. (Ephesians 5:14-15 – KJV)

We can be awake, but sleeping. Paul and Jesus referred to death as 'sleeping.' So if we go back to the beginning and apply the hermeneutical law of first mention, when Adam and Eve sinned, they fell asleep. Yes, they died physically eventually, but death, like every other spiritual principle, has several dimensions or levels of reality. If we are not conscious of God in our day-to-day living, we are sleeping. For those who may be challenged by the word 'consciousness' in this regard, I am referring to our awareness of the reality of God in our lives. Not in the sense that He is somewhere out there and we are isolated from Him, but 'knowing' that He is always present with and in us.

Paul says it this way:

> *And I am convinced that nothing can ever separate us from God's love. Neither death nor life, neither angels nor demons, neither our fears for today nor our worries about tomorrow—not even the powers of hell can separate us from God's love. No power in the sky above or in the earth below—indeed, nothing in all creation will ever be able to separate us from the love of God that is revealed in Christ Jesus our Lord. (Romans 8:38-39 – NLT)*

If that doesn't convince you of God's ever-present nature in your life, then maybe King David's words will:

> If I ascend up into heaven, thou *art* there: if I make my bed in hell, behold, thou *art there*. (Psalm 139:8 – KJV)

Is God in hell? From a purely 'church boy' perspective, I would be afraid to answer yes to that question, but can anything really exist outside of God? It may sound better, to me at least, to say hell is IN God, because there is nothing outside of God.

We need to awaken our consciousness, increase our awareness by our will and faith, that God is always present with us, always working in us, to bring us into the reality of who He made or intended us to be. Most of what we call 'spiritual warfare' is actually a resistance to God. How do I know? Because our lives don't improve, which means we are somehow blocking the process of maturity. We need to start looking for God and seeing God in everything, because He is there.

Prayer:

Father, help me to shift my focus to what is pure, lovely, right, virtuous, of a good report, and worthy of praise. Teach me to engage Your presence more than I engage the kingdom of darkness. I want to turn my focus to You, Lord, to engage Your presence more; to understand the angels who encamp around me more; to learn how to worship You in Spirit and in Truth. May I be aware of Your ever-present nature working in and through me, and may I not stand in the way of whatever 'process' You allow me to go through in order to mature, in Jesus' Name. Amen.

# DAY 15:

# THE KINGDOM OF GOD IS WITHIN (PART 1)

Scripture:

> And when he was demanded of the Pharisees, when the kingdom of God should come, he answered them and said, the kingdom of God cometh not with observation: Neither shall they say, Lo here! or, lo there! for, behold, the kingdom of God is within you. (Luke 17:20-21 – KJV)

Why do Christians live such defeated lives when they have both the Kingdom of God and the Holy Spirit living within them? As believers, we have asked ourselves this question both about ourselves, and others. There are many ways to try to answer that question. This is one way.

We can look at the parables of Jesus regarding the Kingdom of God. For example:

> *Then said he, unto what is the kingdom of God like? and whereunto shall I resemble it? It is like a grain of mustard seed, which a man took, and cast into his garden; and it grew, and waxed a great tree; and the fowls of the air lodged in the branches of it. (Luke 13:18-19 – KJV)*

The mustard seed is the smallest among all seeds. When we get saved, the kingdom of God is deposited in us in seed form, which suggests that it needs to be nurtured and developed until it becomes what it was meant to become. Every seed has within it the full potential of a mature life form that can produce both fruit for those who need it and more seed for the replenishing and expansion of the nature of that one seed. Every human being was also a seed, and that seed had the potential to produce a world changer on the face of the earth; it had the potential to produce you. You have no idea who you are and what you carry inside you.

Our defeat comes from our outward focus. Nothing outside of our being can aid in our growth and maturity. God put everything we need inside, which is why meditation is so important; being still is so important; being quiet is so important. The kingdom of God is inside us, and if we can push past the darkness within by a resilient will and intention, we can connect with what God has put inside us, thereby becoming a well of living water flowing out into the world.

> **Prayer:**
>
> Father, I want to be an agent of change in the world today. I realize that what is in me is greater than anything that is outside of me, so I turn my gaze inward. I see darkness now, but beyond the darkness, I know there is a kingdom of light that I can connect with and partner with to bring light into the darkness in this world. I want to be like You, a light that shines, bringing illumination into the dark areas of creation, in Jesus' Name.

# DAY 16:

# CREATING BALANCE IN THE WORLD

Scripture:

> *For everything there is a season, and a time for every matter under heaven: a time to be born, and a time to die; a time to plant, and a time to pluck up what is planted; a time to kill, and a time to heal; a time to break down, and a time to build up; a time to weep, and a time to laugh; a time to mourn, and a time to dance; a time to cast away stones, and a time to gather stones together; a time to embrace, and a time to refrain from embracing; a time to seek, and a time to lose; a time to keep, and a time to cast away; a time to tear, and a time to sew; a time to keep silence, and a time to speak; a time to love, and a time to hate; a time for war, and a time for peace. (Ecclesiastes 3:1-8 – ESV)*

In talking about balance in our world, God stands as the perfect example because He is, for example, the epitome of both justice and mercy. In answering the question of how God's mercy and justice work together for our salvation, a "Got Questions" article cites:

> God's justice and mercy are seemingly incompatible. After all, justice involves the dispensing of deserved punishment for wrongdoing, and mercy is all about pardon and compassion for an offender. However, these two attributes of God do in fact form a unity within His character.[2]

There is always a demand for balance in our world, which is why we have up and down, east and west, north and south, justice and mercy, life and death. In other words, according to the movie *The Matrix*, there is always an equation trying to balance itself out.

How did Adam and Eve, both made perfect, fall into sin unless the potential for sin was already in them? There was one tree of the knowledge of good and evil. Why wasn't there

---

2   https://www.gotquestions.org/mercy-justice.html

one tree of the knowledge of good and another tree of the knowledge of evil? Why one tree? Why does Paul say that we need to overcome good with evil unless both principles are at work within our being? Church dogma wants us to believe that it's a war against spiritual entities, but Adam didn't have a conversation with a spirit when he chose to disobey God.

We must seek to find a balance in our own lives. If we focus too much on one thing, we tend to throw our equilibrium out of order. If we work hard, we must find time to play. Seek to create a balance in your life, in your thoughts, in how you perceive the world. Even tragedy can sometimes be a way of life trying to balance itself out. God's eyes are always on the good and on the wicked (Proverbs 15:3). He sees all but doesn't always interfere. Learn when to act and when to be still, and in judging others, show mercy.

**Prayer:**

Father, help me to understand the principle of creating a balance in my own life and in the world around me. May I see life and the circumstances I face from Your perspective, and by wisdom, know how to respond to the different challenges I may face as I go through my day. Teach me to deal with difficult people from the perspective of humility, patience, and mercy, and to see my immediate reality through the eyes of heaven, that I may live a balanced life in my thoughts and in my actions, in Jesus' Name. Amen.

# DAY 17:

# THE POWER OF SILENCE

Scripture:

> Be silent in the LORD's presence and wait patiently for him. Don't be angry because of the one whose way prospers or the one who implements evil schemes. (Psalm 37:7 – ISV)

There are different Bible translations that substitute the word 'silence' for words such as 'still, patient, rest, and surrender,' but I like this interpretation. There are other scriptures that speak about being silent before God (See Zephaniah 1:7, Zechariah 2:13, Habakkuk 2:20). There is something about silence, being still, that allows us to enter into a greater spiritual awareness of both ourselves and God, who often speaks in a still, small voice. You can only hear such a voice in silence.

The issue we have is that silence tends to seem contrary to the command that men ought always to pray. I have heard it said by someone I deem to be very wise that every verse of Scripture has at least seventy levels of interpretation. The concept of prayer also has levels of interpretation because it is not just about shouting at the heavens until we lose our voice. There is such a thing as contemplative prayer, and you would be surprised at how powerful this level of prayer is. Most of the prayers I have seen answered in my life are 'heart prayers' that were never uttered from my lips.

One Scriptural example of contemplative prayer is Hannah:

> *And she was in bitterness of soul, and prayed unto the Lord, and wept sore. And she vowed a vow, and said, O Lord of hosts, if thou wilt indeed look on the affliction of thine handmaid, and remember me, and not forget thine handmaid, but wilt give unto thine handmaid a man child, then I will give him unto the Lord all the days of his life, and there shall no razor come upon his head. And it came to pass, as she continued praying before the Lord, that Eli marked her mouth. Now Hannah, she spake in her heart; only*

> *her lips moved, but her voice was not heard: therefore, Eli thought she had been drunken. (1 Samuel 1:11-13 – KJV)*

It was Hannah's womb that bore Samuel, one of the greatest prophets of all time. The Bible says about him, "…none of Samuel's words fall to the ground" (1 Samuel 3:19 – NIV). We can see this from two perspectives. Either Samuel only spoke what the Lord told him to say or Samuel had to be careful what he spoke because the Lord honored every word. If this can be said about Samuel, what about us who are indwelt by the Holy Spirit? We must seek solace in silence and speak only that which we want to see manifested in the world.

### Prayer:

Father, teach me contemplative prayer, to pray from a place of silence, to listen to that small, still voice. Teach me to be still so I can know that You are God, that I may connect with Your presence within me. Help me to know when to be silent and know when to speak and what to speak, in Jesus' Name.

# DAY 18:

# EYES TO SEE

Scripture:

> The eyes of your understanding being enlightened; that ye may know what is the hope of his calling, and what the riches of the glory of his inheritance in the saints, and what is the exceeding greatness of his power to us-ward who believe, according to the working of his mighty power, which he wrought in Christ, when he raised him from the dead, and set him at his own right hand in the heavenly places. (Ephesians 1:18-20 – KJV)

This is one of my favorite texts, and I have yet to grasp experientially the fullness of what Paul is saying here, but I like his use of the word 'understanding' because it speaks to us taking hold of Truth.

We often view the Word and the world through the eyes of skepticism, and we are quick to shut things down because we are uncomfortable with it or it just doesn't sound right. My spiritual growth did not begin until I grasped the idea that there is truth at the foundation of everything, and if I look at the worst things long enough, I will be able to pull the seed of truth embedded in it. In this text, Paul uses the word 'enlightened,' which is actually a powerful word. The enlightened are those who are able to see. The suggestion here is that most of us cannot see, and by seeing, I mean into the realm of the spirit.

Paul gives a long list in this text, none of which we can come into unless our 'eyes' are open. Unless our spiritual eyes, or the eyes of our soul/spirit, are open, we cannot know the hope of Jesus' calling, the riches of the glory of His inheritance, or His great power at work within us. The prerequisite to this understanding is enlightenment. One must be able to see in order to understand, so our greatest need and prayer in this season should be for God to give us eyes to see.

**Prayer:**

Father, thank You for Truth. I pray that the eyes of my understanding be open NOW to know what is the hope of Your calling, and the riches of the glory of Your inheritance in the saints, and what is the exceeding greatness of Your power to us who believe, according to the working of Your mighty power which was wroth in Christ when You raised Him from the dead and seated Him at Your right hand, in Jesus' Name. Amen.

# DAY 19:

# THE CURRENCY OF A SUPERNATURAL LIFE

Scripture:

> And he said unto them, Why are ye so fearful? How is it that ye have no faith? (Mark 4:40 – KJV)

The world and our existence seem to be built on the principle of trading. We cannot get anything without it costing us something. And even the things that are purported as 'free' can actually cost more than what we intentionally pay for. Faith is the currency of the supernatural. It draws what is in the supernal realm into the realm of physicality. There is no substitute for faith.

The absence of faith allows for the disease of fear to multiply in our lives, as we see in the story told in Mark 4. The Disciples were all on a ship, and Jesus was asleep. They woke Him up, and He rebuked the winds and they dissipated. He then turned to them and scolded them for not having faith. If you read the text carefully, you will see that 'no faith' is attributed to 'not trying.' They didn't even conceive of the thought that they had the authority to speak to the winds. Little faith is attributed to those who try but don't get the desired result. Great faith refers to those who relentlessly go after something without backing down until the desired result is realized.

Which category do you fall in today? Are you among those who 'don't try' or those who 'try and fail?' Maybe you are counted among the few who refuse to back down until the desired outcome is manifested. We have this divine privilege to choose which category we place ourselves in. Faith is a personal choice. You have it because every believer is given a measure of faith by God (See Romans 12:3). How you use your divine currency is entirely up to you, but if you want to bring anything from heaven to earth, it cannot be done by ritualistic, mechanical prayer; by following traditions and rituals; or even by a well-planned church service. All things are possible to him who believes. Faith is the only prerequisite to a supernatural lifestyle. Faith is all you need to get God's attention.

> **Prayer:**
>
> Father, thank You that You have deposited in me a measure of faith. You said even if my faith is only as small as the smallest seed, I would be able to speak to mountains and see them removed. I thank You that such faith is in me and ask that You aid me in exercising my faith so I can experience daily manifestations of Your divine presence and glory in and around my life, in Jesus' Name.

# DAY 20:

# WHEN OUR FAITH DOESN'T WORK

Scripture:

> Then came the disciples to Jesus apart, and said, why could not we cast him out? And Jesus said unto them, because of your unbelief: for verily I say unto you, if ye have faith as a grain of mustard seed, ye shall say unto this mountain, remove hence to yonder place; and it shall remove; and nothing shall be impossible unto you. Howbeit this kind goeth not out but by prayer and fasting. (Matthew 17:19-21 – KJV)

In this text, it would seem that Jesus is referring to prayer and fasting as a prerequisite to casting out a demon. If this was true, and considering that most of our churches fast and pray every week, then we should see greater manifestations of God's glory in our midst. Is it possible that we are missing something?

Let's look again at the text. Why couldn't the disciples drive out the demon? Jesus says it was because of their unbelief. The problem was not a lack of fasting and prayer, but unbelief. It is safe to say, then, that the 'this kind' that needs to go by prayer and fasting was 'unbelief.'

It is not a lack of faith that blocks us from manifesting anything from heaven here on earth; it is the presence of unbelief. Paul says God has given to every believer a measure of faith (Romans 12:3), so where does this unbelief come from? Why do we approach God with such uncertainty, skepticism, and fear when He assures us that we can come to Him with confidence, knowing He will give us what we desire?

Faith is a choice, incumbent to our will. We choose to believe or not to believe because the potential for both faith and unbelief exists simultaneously within our being. If we are sick and we believe that God will heal us, that faith will produce some corresponding action. Our inaction then can be linked to our choice to not exercise faith, but sometimes we make the leap and it still doesn't produce the desired result.

I believe the disciples were still at the stage in their spiritual development where they were trying to determine what the 'formula' for miracles was. They tried to cast out the demon but watched to see if what they were doing would work. Their formula didn't work, and they asked Jesus why it didn't work. Unbelief forces the one who acts to watch and see if God will do what He says. Faith knows it is already done.

> **Prayer:**
>
> Father, thank You for Your Word – the potency of what You have spoken that can never be undermined. You call us to believe You, to exercise faith, so I come in agreement that Your will be done on earth as it is in heaven. I declare it, I believe it, and I call it to be so. And in like manner, as one man once prayed and received the miracle he desired, so too I pray, "Lord, I believe, help thou my unbelief," in Jesus' Name. Amen.

# DAY 21:

# THE KINGDOM OF GOD IS WITHIN (PART 2)

Scripture:

> But seek ye first the **kingdom of God**, and his righteousness; and all these things shall be added unto you. (Matthew 6:33 – KJV)

If we are called to seek first the kingdom of God, and the Kingdom of God is within each believer, then the first stop for every new believer is within him/herself. We have not taught this principle very well as a church, and because the 'other' religions and cults have this inner focus, we think it is a bad thing and worthy of being avoided, but that is to our detriment. Even non-believers have something inside themselves that they can tap into to become a greater version of themselves. Believers have something greater; both must look within.

What I find a little scary is that we can lose that which we ignore:

> *Therefore say I unto you, The **kingdom of God** shall be taken from you, and given to a nation bringing forth the fruits thereof. (Matthew 21:43 – KJV)*

The Kingdom of God is given as a seed, and by looking within, by our own gaze from a divine perspective, the seed will come to fruition. It is from this perspective that we are able to bear fruit that remains (John 15:15).

One of the issues we face today as believers that cause our spiritual growth to be stunted is that we grew up in an environment that taught us to focus externally. We are always looking for the answers outside of ourselves when what we truly seek is already deposited within by God Himself. The same principle was at work when Moses went to cry out to God about being trapped between a mountain, the Red Sea, and the bloodthirsty Egyptians in pursuit. Moses already had what he needed to bring deliverance to the children of Israel. He just needed to be told or reminded. Likewise, you have the kingdom of God within you, and that is all you need to change this world. Turn your gaze inward until you begin to see the potential and power that resides there.

> **Prayer:**
>
> Father, thank You that I have been given all spiritual blessings in heavenly realms in Christ. Thank You that I have what I need to replenish this world and impact lives for Your glory. Thank You that I have the kingdom of God within me. Help me to connect with it, to be absorbed by it, and to partner with it in bringing light and transformation to this world, in Jesus' Name. Amen.

# DAY 22:

# EXPECTATION VERSUS FAITH

~

Scripture:

> For the earnest expectation of the creature waiteth for the manifestation of the sons of God. (Romans 8:19 – KJV)

Expectation is an interesting word that I hear being used a lot in most supernatural circles. We are told to enter God's presence with expectation. If we desire a miracle, we are advised to come and be prayed for with expectation. The problem I have with the word is that expectation often leads to disappointment and discouragement. So I keep wondering, is it really a good thing?

The word 'expectation' is found fourteen times in the King James Version. Here is one instance:

> For the earnest expectation of the creature waiteth for the

> manifestation of the sons of God. For the creature was made subject to vanity, not willingly, but by reason of him who hath subjected the same in hope, Because the creature itself also shall be delivered from the bondage of corruption into the glorious liberty of the children of God. (Romans 8:19-21)

I like the word 'earnest' because it changes the nature of 'expectation.' It speaks to a consistent yearning for something that ends with the fulfillment of what one is expecting. Some of the other uses of the word 'expectation' in Scripture is in the context that if a desired outcome is not realized, then there is embarrassment and disappointment. If you have ever been bold enough to pray for a miracle with great expectation and not see it happen, then you know what I am talking about. Expectation is not faith; it actually questions one's reality. The purpose of expectation is to provoke us to realize that there is an exception to the rule, another way, other options to consider, more to our existence than our present experiences try to convince us to believe.

When John the Baptist was put in prison, he sent someone to ask Jesus, *"Are you the Messiah we've been expecting or should we keep looking for someone else?"* (Matthew 11:3 – NLT). So many people missed the Messiah because He didn't fit their expectation. Expectation does not guarantee manifestation, but it does make us aware of the options available. We must be careful not to confuse expectation with faith. Expectation can lead to disappointments, but faith always produces fruit.

> But without faith it is impossible to please *him*: for he that cometh to God must believe that he is, and *that* he is a rewarder of them that diligently seek him. (Hebrews 11:6 – KJV)

**Prayer:**

Father, while I approach You this day with expectation in my heart, may I not allow my expected outcome to override my faith. You have called me to believe You, and it is that faith in who You are that produces manifestations, miracles, signs, and wonders and not an expectation of what You will do in response to my assumed needs. Help me to love You and exercise faith, irrespective of the outcome, in Jesus' Name. Amen.

# DAY 23:

# OVERCOMING THE ENEMY (SELF)

Scripture:

> And when he had called the people unto him with his disciples also, he said unto them, Whosoever will come after me, let him deny himself, and take up his cross, and follow me. (Mark 8:34 – KJV)

The human will is more powerful than we give it credit for. There is no force in the universe that can get us to do what we don't want to do. God is all-powerful, yet He created human beings with the capacity to walk away from Him, even deny that He exists, and He can choose not to impose His will on any man.

When Jesus walked this earth as a man, many people followed Him because of what He did, yet He turned to those same people and said before they could follow Him, they must first deny themselves, then take up their cross. Do you realize that Jesus said that long before He had to walk the long road to Golgotha with a cross on His back? The symbolism of His prophetic word here is profound.

The Scriptures cite four things that we must overcome in order to begin to walk out the reality of who we are and experience the transformation that Christ made available to us:

1. A world of tribulation (John 16:33)
2. The wicked one (1 John 2:13-14)
3. The spirits of false prophets (1 John 4:1-5)
4. The spirits of antichrist (1 John 4:1-5)

The concept of overcoming speaks to our capacity to make that which appears at first to be a hindrance completely irrelevant. It is not a constant engaging of spiritual opposition (what we call spiritual warfare), for once you overcome such forces, they cease to be relevant in your life. Also, because of the power of our will, we can become an adversary (satan) to ourselves. Our 'self' can be our greatest hindrance and therefore must be 'denied.' In other words, we can become 'a wicked one.' A denial of self renders it powerless to stop our progress and growth, for it is indeed impossible for one to take up any cross, let alone follow Christ to death, if self has a say in the matter.

> **Prayer:**
>
> Father, I humbly come before You with a request on my lips that You would teach me to walk the path Jesus walked, to endure the pains He endured, and to bask in the glory that He enjoyed. I say, like Paul, that I may know You, the power of Your resurrection and the fellowship of Your suffering until I am conformed to Your image and likeness. May I overcome as Jesus overcame; may I gain victory over self, the wicked one, and the world, in Jesus' Name. Amen.

# DAY 24:

# UNION WITH GOD

Scripture:

> That they all may be one; as thou, Father, art in me, and I in thee, that they also may be one in us: that the world may believe that thou hast sent me. And the glory which thou gavest me I have given them; that they may be one, even as we are one: I in them, and thou in me, that they may be made perfect in one; and that the world may know that thou hast sent me, and hast loved them, as thou hast loved me. (John 17:21-23 – KJV)

I grew up in church (30+ years) and I don't remember hearing a message preached on this passage of Scripture. The church may even say union with God is impossible because we are too vile and savage. Let me push this a little further. Jesus' prayer continued:

> *Father, I will that they also, whom thou hast given me, be with me where I am; that they may behold my glory, which thou hast given me: for thou lovedst me before the foundation of the world. (John 17:24 – KJV)*

I found this verse interesting, considering what Paul said:

> *And hath raised us up together, and made us sit together in heavenly places in Christ Jesus. (Ephesians 2:6 – KJV)*

This sounds to me like the answer to Jesus' prayer. So, my question is, what is your location? Do you realize that your salvation experience was your first death (see Romans 6:8). Now this verse should make a little more sense to you:

> *He that hath an ear, let him hear what the Spirit saith unto the churches; He that overcometh shall not be hurt of the second death. (Revelation 2:11 – KJV)*

So, why are you worried about death? Why allow the fear of death to cripple your life? Your salvation experience propelled you into 'union with God,' you are just not conscious of it. You have forgotten who you are and where you are located. You think you are on earth striving to get into heaven, but you are already with Jesus. You are one with God – that's what the Scripture says, right? Do you really want to spend your life reminding God of how unworthy and vile you are and fighting demons? Don't you think a more fitting endeavor would be just to enjoy God's presence and be saturated by His love?

**Prayer:**

Father, thank You for the redemption that came through Christ's willingness to suffer and die on the Cross. As He hung on the Cross, He declared, "It is finished." I declare that now over my life, "It is indeed finished." You have paid the price that I might be redeemed, that I may once again be restored to my rightful place in God, in complete union. I am in Christ, Christ is in God, I am in God – no separation, no disconnection. Father, may Your life, essence, nature, and influence flow through me into the world, as it did through Christ, in Jesus' Name.

# DAY 25:

# SHIFTING PERSPECTIVE – RENEWING THE MIND

Scripture:

> And be not conformed to this world: but be ye transformed by the renewing of your mind, that ye may prove what is that good, and acceptable, and perfect, will of God. (Romans 12:2 – KJV)

The transformation of our minds through renewal is not a one-time event, and neither is it an automatic process. It is a continual and deliberate attempt to allow ourselves to receive a new revelation. If what you believe now and your interpretation of Scripture today is the same as it was ten years ago, or even three months ago, then you have not allowed yourself to be inducted in the mind renewal process.

I am amazed at the culture we have developed where we like to hear what we already know. What is the point of that? It was uncomfortable for me at first to expose myself to unfamiliar teachings, but I learned to look into the matter and realized that from a biblical perspective, a lot of it made sense. There is no one interpretation of Scripture. The Word of God is spirit and life, and it has the capacity to reveal its meaning based on one's level of maturity. Our ability to submit to the mind renewal process is the determining factor in moving to higher levels of learning and experience. The suggestion here is that you can get stuck in kindergarten, repeating the same grade, if you don't accept the reality that there is a new revelation waiting to take you to a new dimension in Christ.

God is deliberate in what He created. He hides Himself even in the basic things of life. As it is above, so it is below. For example, babies must be cared for and nurtured until they become conscious of their existence. Then, they must be taught based on their level of maturity. The concept of teaching is a principle that allows the mind to grow as the body grows. When we are born again, the same principle applies. There is no growth without a teacher, and when you go to a new grade, everything you are taught is a new revelation. Our perspective shifts and our mind is renewed each time we assimilate new revelation when it comes.

> **Prayer:**
>
> Father, forgive my reluctance to accept new revelation. Pardon my skepticism and resistance to new information that makes me uncomfortable. I realize now that in order to be transformed by the renewing of my mind, I must go through discomfort as my mind is forced to release old information in order to embrace new revelation. I pray that all the opportunities lost for me to grow because of my resistance may pass my way again and that I will be more open to receive Your Word, whether it be for correction, for reproof, or for edification. Lord, I am open to what You want to reveal to me in this season, in Jesus' Name.

# DAY 26:

# UNTETHERING FROM THE CHURCH SYSTEM

Scripture:

> And let us consider how we may spur one another on toward love and good deeds, not giving up meeting together, as some are in the habit of doing, but encouraging one another—and all the more as you see the Day approaching. (Hebrews 10:24-25 – NIV)

When the Word of God became flesh and dwelt among humanity, there was a church in existence. They believed strongly in the law and the prophets. They adored Moses for what he had done and accomplished in God on their behalf. They met weekly in the synagogue for worship, prayer, and the reading of Scripture. They tithed, they fasted, and they demonstrated levels of commitment to God that we may not be familiar with today. Yet not one of the chosen twelve disciples came from the church. As a matter of fact, the church was hostile toward Jesus. Very few members of the church system then paid any attention to who Jesus proclaimed to be.

We can be so engrafted in a church system that we fail to nourish and develop a personal walk with God. Most churches are designed to be performance-based and activity driven. We 'do' church instead of 'being' the church. The language of our day is still "Let's go to church." As I studied Scripture carefully, I began to accept the organic nature of the church and my induction as a member of the body of Christ. I began to resist the structural demands of an institutional establishment that feeds on performance, irrespective of our spiritual maturity. I wanted to be more than just a pawn on a religious chessboard. But I needed to be untethered from a system that bounded me while trying to convince me that I was free.

Church was never meant to become an enslaving principle for believers, using a language of fear and death to increase our numbers so we can give a nice report. Church is meant to be a body of people who would be responsible for each other and grow together to maturity. It is a body of people who could confess their faults to each other, pray, and receive healing. It is a body that understands that Christ is the head, not a pastor, and each member plays a significant role in activating and advancing the kingdom of God within each of us. We must cease from *doing* church and start *being* the church. For most of us, that will demand a season of untethering so we can be released from faulty thinking, the doctrine of men, the demands of ministerial and position responsibilities above loving God and people, and the idea that we must earn our salvation.

**Prayer:**

Father, I repent for *doing* church instead of *being* the church. I accept Your Word, that I am a valuable member of the body of Christ on earth and have a significant role to play in activating and advancing the kingdom of God within me. Help me to change my language from speaking of the church as an external institution to honoring the church as the body of believers, called, anointed, and appointed for such a time as this. I want to be known as the Church and manifest Your glory and presence wherever I am in the world, in Jesus' Name. Amen.

# DAY 27:

# UNTETHERING FROM THE WORLD SYSTEM

Scripture:

> Love not the world, neither the things that are in the world. If any man love the world, the love of the Father is not in him. (1 John 2:15 – KJV)

Many established systems in our world are designed to keep us in a non-progressive cycle. There is the medical system. When one gets sick, their first recourse is to seek medical assistance. They take the prescribed medication, or try to self-assess their symptoms with the help of Dr. Google and buy over-the-counter medicine. If something goes amiss in the body, then a surgery becomes highly recommended, and this system thrives on the fear of death. The medical system saves lives and takes lives, but it is still seen as a priority in dealing with the human body.

Then there is the financial system. Here we are employed with a salary that can barely cover our expenses to go to work, buy our daily necessities, raise children, own a home and car, and cover a budget for entertainment. We are underqualified for a good salary but overqualified to get loans and credit cards that end up enslaving us within the system. We are unable to break free or even leave a less-than-satisfying job because of the fear that we may lose our house, car, and comfort.

There is the peer system, where everyone tries to get everyone else to do the same thing, perform at the same level, own the same possessions, act the same, dress the same, talk the same and repeat the same mistakes.

There is the religious system, where the battle for who is right continues, and we become judge, jury, and executioner of each other's religious persuasion and convictions. Within this system, position is power, and it is used as a tool to control people and get them to conform to one's way of thinking.

It is hard to be in this world, with all its demands, and not be influenced to participate in one system or the other. We need money, so we must work because the two other alternatives to getting paid are to steal or beg. One of the goals of maturing as a child of God is learning to untether from the systems of the world. It takes intention, determination, and sacrifice. Jesus paid tax from a fish's mouth. The citizens of heaven really don't need the systems of this world as a source, because they have access to a higher medical, financial, and religious/spiritual system that we should actually be superimposing on what exists in our world today. We were born again from another world. We need to wake up to the reality of who we are, tap into the divine potential within us to create new systems in the world, and untether from the broken ones.

**Prayer:**

Father, thank You that I am born from another world and that there are divine systems from which my daily needs can be sourced. Give me this day my daily bread, that I may not be in want. I declare healing and restoration to my body, to every organ, every bone, every sinew. I speak the life of Jesus Christ into them and command every cell to be well and every organ to function at optimal level. Help me, Lord, to be more responsible with my finances, to give freely and cheerfully, to walk in prosperity and divine health. I turn to You as my source and turn away from the systems of this world that seek to bind me in a non-progressive cycle. May I prosper and be in good health as my soul prospers, In Jesus' Name.

# DAY 28:

# WALKING IN THE SPIRIT

Scripture:

> *This I say then, walk in the Spirit, and ye shall not fulfil the lust of the flesh. (Galatians 5:16 – KJV)*

Close your eyes for two minutes, observe, then open them and continue reading. In those two minutes, what you were looking at is the realm of the spirit. Most of us see darkness when our eyes are closed, which means we have not yet developed the capacity to see. Spiritual sight is every believer's inheritance. The problem is nobody taught us this when we were born again.

When babies are born, their eyes are open, but they have no idea what they are looking at because they don't have a reference for what they see. Similarly, with our eyes closed, because we don't have a reference for what we are seeing, it appears as darkness. We cannot walk in the Spirit unless we can see in the Spirit. We can be led by the Spirit, but very often we really don't know which kind of spirit is giving us direction. Our incapacity to see causes a lot of confusion in our churches. Just imagine a blind guy walking down an unfamiliar street.

Paul cites 'walking in the Spirit' as the antidote to not fulfilling the lust of the flesh. It is more than just trying to will ourselves not to do something wrong, reading the Bible, praying, fasting, tithing, going to church – you can do all that, and so much more, and still be a slave to your flesh. Something is missing. Our spiritual eyes need to be opened, and I am not just talking about dreams and imagination. In the natural, you would not attempt to walk unless you could see. For example, you have been through your house a million times. You know where everything is. Try walking in your house with your eyes closed and using only your imagination.

We must develop our spiritual sight so we can effectively walk in the Spirit. It will take practice. It is good to hear, and hearing can help to develop sight, but it is far better to see. Jesus said: *"I tell you the truth: the Son can do nothing on his own; he does only what he sees his Father doing. What the Father does, the Son also does" (John 5:19 – KJV).* This is the legacy and inheritance of all believers.

> **Prayer:**
>
> Father, I pray for eyes to see so I will be capable of obeying Your command to walk in the Spirit. May the mystery hidden in the darkness begin to be revealed to me as I seek to walk as Jesus walked and do as Jesus did. The promise is that I will be capable of doing even greater things, so, Father, I don't want to walk in ignorance. I don't want to be counted among the blind who are trying to lead the blind. Help me to see, give me a reference for what I am seeing, teach me the mysteries of Your kingdom. Let me experience Your glory by truly walking in the Spirit, in Jesus' Name.

# DAY 29:

# TAKING YOUR SEAT WITH CHRIST

Scripture:

> And hath raised us up together, and made us sit together in heavenly places in Christ Jesus. (Ephesians 2:6 – KJV)

The first book I read about heaven was by Randy Alcorn. It was great, but nothing compared to what I know about heaven now. I always questioned how the men and women of the Bible were able to have such profound, spiritual experiences, but I understand now that they had access to something that we have access to in an even greater measure today because Jesus came and restored all things.

We have talked about Jesus' prayer in the Book of John, that we be with Him where He is. So, where is Jesus now? If you said everywhere, then you are correct. If Jesus is everywhere, and we are with Him because we died, rose, and ascended with Him when we became born again, then where are we? We were wrong to put heaven in the future when Jesus made it a reality for us now.

A couple of years ago, a great supernatural move began. In our history, we have seen isolated pockets of this occurrence, but the move would die with the people at the helm. This time, the *'anointing'* was spreading like wildfire, as if a whole bunch of people from across the globe was just waking up to the supernatural reality. The term *'bringing heaven to earth'* was coined, and it became a thing. Many churches use it in their Sunday morning language today.

Paul is explicit when he talks about our identity and position in Christ. He had the experience of being caught up, and while he shared so little with us, I believe he fulfilled his goal to make us conscious of the fact that we can be caught up too. He says we are already there. A seat has been prepared for you, and all you need to do is take your seat. If you can't see, do it by faith. And by faith, live from that place. Train yourself to consciously speak and think from that place. I promise if you practice this daily, it will change your life by opening realms and dimensions of possibilities you never thought possible.

> **Prayer:**
>
> Father, I thank You that when Jesus died, I died. When He was buried, I was buried. When He was raised from the dead, I was raised from the dead. When He ascended, I ascended, and I am seated with Christ. I thank You that where Jesus is, I am also there. I ask now that You would make me conscious of this reality. Allow me to see, hear, and know by virtue of my true identity in Christ. I take my seat with Him, by faith, in Jesus' Name.

# DAY 30:

# IMMORTALITY NOW

Scripture:

> And he said unto them, Verily I say unto you, that there be some of them that stand here, which shall not taste of death, till they have seen the kingdom of God come with power. (Mark 9:1 - KJV)

I was in meditation one evening, contemplating my own life, when the word *"immortality"* crept into my thoughts. It was an interesting experience, and I started to delve in the matter. One verse that caught my attention is the one quoted above in Mark 9:1. Here are a few others:

> And it came to pass, as they still went on, and talked, that, behold, there appeared a chariot of fire, and horses of fire, and parted them both asunder; and Elijah went up by a whirlwind into heaven. (2 Kings 2:11 – KJV)

> And all the days of Enoch were three hundred sixty and five years: And Enoch walked with God: and he was not; for God took him. (Genesis 5:23-24 - KJV)

> And, behold, the veil of the temple was rent in twain from the top to the bottom; and the earth did quake, and the rocks rent; and the graves were opened; and many bodies of the saints which slept arose, and came out of the graves after his resurrection, and went into the holy city, and appeared unto many. (Matthew 27:51-53 – KJV)

> And whosoever liveth and believeth in me shall never die. Believest thou this? (John 11:26 – KJV)

Believest thou what is written? It is clear to me that believers have access to immortality now. Paul says, *"For this corruptible must put on incorruption, and this mortal must put on immortality" (1 Corinthians 15:53 – KJV).* He didn't say we must die a physical death for it to happen.

If believers have access to immortality now, and not everyone is destined to die, why does life demonstrate a different reality? I realize by observation that we have developed a language of death. Christians generally prepare for two things, the return of Christ (Rapture) and their physical death, whichever comes first. If the rapture is a faulty interpretation of Scripture, then there is only one thing left to prepare for.

I have been a part of the same church for over thirty years. I have seen many of our church mothers and fathers die, and this is the trend. They serve the church faithfully for many years, suffer from some debilitating disease for the latter part of their lives, and then they die. Jesus promises a reward in this life and the one to come for our sacrifices (See Mark 10:29-30), and I don't think He was referring to *'church work'* as the sacrifice. It can be, but it is not really – not in the context of what we call *'church'* now anyway.

We need to intentionally develop a language of life. My earthly father believed that he would live to be seventy years, and by reason of strength, eighty. He made that declaration throughout his entire life. He died a couple days before his eighty-first birthday. Stop going into your future by thought and declaration and planting death there. Put life and immortality there instead and you may just live long enough to fulfill your destiny, or until God decides to move you from this realm to another supernaturally. Some of us will die; some of us will not. You do have a say in the matter.

> Prayer:
>
> Father, what can I say but thanks. You have opened up realms of possibility for Your most prized creation. We have allowed our identity to be lost and end up wandering around the wilderness mindlessly and in ignorance. You have made us kings and priests and have restored all that was lost, including immortality. I declare that I shall live and not die. I shall be translated and not buried. I shall change from mortal to immortality, in the twinkling of an eye, while living in this body, in Jesus' Name.

# DAY 31:

# TO HIM WHO OVERCOMES

Scripture:

> And he that overcometh, and keepeth my works unto the end, to him will I give power over the nations. (Revelation 2:26 – KJV)

Those who have military and athletic training have a better grasp of what advancing the kingdom of God demands than mere civilians. Obstacles are seen as something to overcome, not as deterrents to progress, in order to step into a greater dimension of their training. What we go through in life is designed to shift us into a greater understanding of who we are once we overcome it. The life of a maturing believer is filled with opportunities for overcoming. Consider these Scriptures:

> My brethren, count it all joy when ye fall into divers temptations; knowing this, that the trying of

> your faith worketh patience. But let patience have her perfect work, that ye may be perfect and entire, wanting nothing. (James 1:2-4 – KJV)
>
> And not only so, but we glory in tribulations also: knowing that tribulation worketh patience; and patience, experience; and experience, hope: and hope maketh not ashamed; because the love of God is shed abroad in our hearts by the Holy Ghost which is given unto us. (Romans 5:3-5 – KJV)

Overcoming is the technology for accessing the kingdom of God within. The life that is free from challenges lacks the veracity of spiritual growth. It is one way to move from one level to the next. Why do you think Jesus had to suffer and die in order to access salvation for humanity? What are you willing to go through to access salvation for your own family? Jesus even said our willingness to lay down our lives was the greatest act of love. We must stop being afraid to go through difficult times. We must stop being afraid of trauma, bad news, calamity, suffering, and persecution, because there is a seed of life embedded within these things, and only those who go through them have access to the fruit of that seed.

Salvation is not the only determining factor of where we find ourselves when we leave this realm. We must answer the question, *"What have you overcome in your earthly life?"* Even Jesus had to give an answer. Don't spend your life trying to avoid calamity and turning your eyes away from what is difficult to look at. If I were you, I would pray for God to put greater obstacles in your path, because the technology of overcoming is what makes you more than a conqueror (Romans 8:37) and qualifies you to be appointed a king over nations in the world to come.

Prayer:

Father, thank You for all the troubles I have faced, and will face, in this life. Give me the will and tenacity to go through any storms You allow to come my way, believing that there is a greater version of myself waiting on the other side. I don't want to go around it, and I don't want to go over it. You know the degree to which I am able to bear, so as I determine in my heart to go through whatever You allow, give me strength and the assurance that You are with me throughout it all. I know Your plans for me are perfect – they are plans of peace and prosperity, to bring me over into an expected end, so Father, with all my heart, despite my calamity and the trauma set in my path, I make this declaration now that I will trust You to the end, I will praise You in spite of, and I will keep my heart still and my eyes on You until I overcome, in Jesus' Name.

# ABOUT THE AUTHOR

C. Orville McLeish is a published Inspirational Author, Screenwriter, and Playwright. He is the founder and CEO of the Heart of a Christian Playwright and HCP Book Publishing. He is from a Pentecostal background, born and raised in the Church of God of Prophecy. He is a gifted young man, called to pursue a more Mystical version of Christianity, and seeks to educate anyone who will listen on their true identity in Christ Jesus.

Connect with me:

Amazon Author Page: https://www.amazon.com/C-Orville-McLeish/e/B08TCFD8KR

Author Website: https://corvillemcleish.com/

Goodreads: https://www.goodreads.com/author/show/17913132.C_Orville_McLeish

Facebook: https://www.facebook.com/authorcorvillemcleish/

Instagram: https://www.instagram.com/cleveland.mcleish/

Linkedin: https://www.linkedin.com/in/author-c-orville-mcleish-98316333/

Twitter: https://twitter.com/HCP_Ministries

Please leave an honest Book Review on my Amazon Page. I would really appreciate it.

Shalom.

www.ingramcontent.com/pod-product-compliance
Lightning Source LLC
Chambersburg PA
CBHW052200110526
44591CB00012B/2017